THE NEW LIFE LIBRARY

INSTANT STRETCHES

FOR STRESS RELIEF

INSTANT ENERGY
AND RELAXATION
WITH EASY-TO-FOLLOW
YOGA STRETCHING
TECHNIQUES

MARK EVANS

SPECIAL PHOTOGRAPHY
DON LAST

Sebastian Kelly

This Paperback edition published by
Sebastian Kelly
2 Rectory Road, Oxford OX4 1BW

Produced by Anness Publishing Limited
Hermes House, 88-89 Blackfriars Road, London SE1 8HA

A CIP catalogue record for this book is available from the British Library

ISBN 1 84081 384 9

Publisher: Joanna Lorenz
Editor: Fiona Eaton
Designer: Bobbie Colgate Stone
Photographer: Don Last

Printed and bound in Singapore

© Anness Publishing Limited 1996
Updated © 1999
3 5 7 9 10 8 6 4 2

Publisher's note:
The reader should not regard the recommendations, ideas and techniques expressed and
described in this book as substitutes for the advice of a qualified medical practitioner or other
qualified professional. Any use to which the recommendations, ideas and techniques are put is
at the reader's sole discretion and risk.

CONTENTS

INTRODUCTION

HAVE YOU EVER watched a cat waking up? More often than not, it will give an exaggerated yawn, then arch its back until stretched to its limit, before loosely letting go and gracefully moving off on its way. Have you ever stopped to wonder why it makes these movements? The cat knows instinctively the value of stretching in maintaining flexibility and improving circulation to the muscles; you too can become stronger and more flexible with regular stretching exercises.

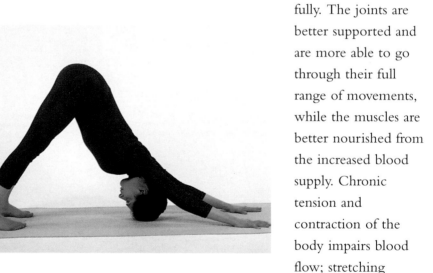

Most of us tend to hold in patterns of tension arising from everyday cares and worries, bad posture, lack of exercise and so on. These patterns make us feel stiff and unbending, and directly interfere with our movements. Inflexibility within our bodies can in turn affect mental flexibility, and we can become stuck in thought as well as in action. Regular stretching exercises not only free our bodies, allowing us to move easily, but can also help us to think and act without being so restricted.

By stretching muscles, ligaments and tendons, we make them stronger. The lengthening actions help us to stand and walk taller and more gracefully. The joints are better supported and are more able to go through their full range of movements, while the muscles are better nourished from the increased blood supply. Chronic tension and contraction of the body impairs blood flow; stretching improves this, giving added vigour and vitality.

Stretching is not a new idea; for centuries it has formed an essential part of the physical exercises that are one aspect of yoga. Yoga is an ancient Indian system of self-improvement, embracing the body, mind and spirit. It is not a

religion, but is indeed a way of life for thousands of people who put its ideas into practice on a daily basis. The physical exercises, including breathing techniques and meditation, have become highly popular in the West in recent decades. There are yoga classes in almost every town, and the best way to learn about the exercises is from a trained, supportive teacher. This book is not meant in any way to be a substitute for such classes, but gives practical, simple suggestions for stretching that you can easily put into practice at home.

The benefits of yoga stretches derive from the slowness of the movements and holding the positions. They do not strain the heart but help to relieve tension and strain, and conserve energy. The stretches in this book are not all from yoga by any means, but they follow its principles to exercise the muscles gently. We have tried not to suggest complicated movements that look impossibly difficult. Never overdo a movement or strain to stretch – you should enjoy it. Stretching is for everyone: all ages can benefit from it, and we can all improve our flexibility.

CAUTION:

The stretching exercises suggested in this book are intended as a general guide to movements for increasing flexibility, improving muscle tone and circulation, and helping to maintain good posture. Clearly, they are not a substitute for individual advice or good yoga or exercise classes, and if you are in any doubt about how to do an exercise, or whether it is suitable for you, seek advice from a qualified teacher.

If you have any physical health problems, such as a back injury, or suffer from a medical condition that gives rise to worry about doing any of the stretches, you should seek medical advice.

For some conditions, such as high blood pressure or thyroid problems, inverted postures such as the "Plough" are contra-indicated.

If you have not done any exercise for a while, start stretching gently and build up your flexibility gradually. Easing out tension through stretching can make muscles ache at first, but none of these exercises should be painful: stop if there is acute discomfort. In the main, you should feel only benefit from including some stretching in your daily life, becoming more energized, supple and improving your posture. It's always wise to remember, however, if in doubt, don't do it.

PREPARATION

ONE OF THE BEST THINGS about stretches is that you can do some simple exercises anywhere, at any time: at home, in the office, standing in a queue or even sitting in the car. However, in order to get the most benefit from regular stretching, and particularly yoga practice, it is important to create a quiet, comfortable space and to give yourself the time to do the movements without pressure or interruptions. Making this space, both literally and in the busy schedule of the day, is in itself a relaxing, unwinding step and will enhance the effectiveness of the actual exercises.

Ideally, make an area that feels quiet and calming to you, perhaps with softer lighting if it is needed at all, maybe with a mat for the floor-based stretches. If you have any back discomfort, or just need extra support when lying down, then a couple of cushions may be useful. It is helpful to wear loose clothing so that you

can move freely and easily. If the weather permits try to let in some fresh air – but do not get cold: these exercises are not intended to work up a sweat or strain the heart, but to make you less stiff and tense, and generally more flexible.

Yoga exercises are best learnt in a class with an experienced teacher; for maximum benefit, however, a regular practice time between classes is important. This book is mainly concerned with stretching exercises that you can do on your own, for self-help with relaxation. If you become inspired to take up more of these postures, do find a good, local class – and also create a little environment at home in which you can enjoy stretching or yoga regularly.

You may find that your partner, family or friends want to stretch with you; use these exercises to release tensions, improve circulation, tone your body and have fun as you stretch.

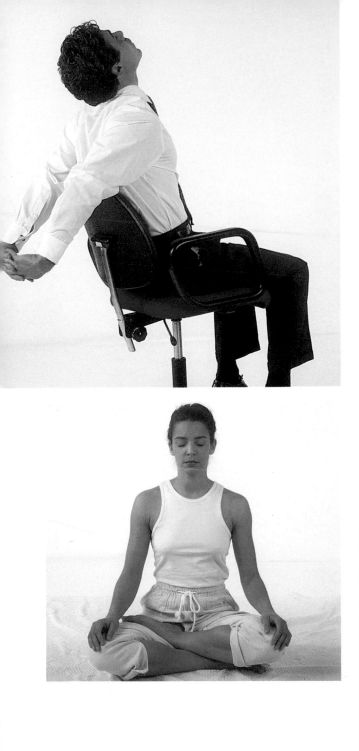

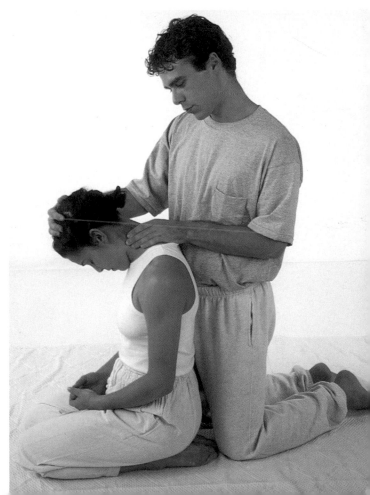

WARM-UP EXERCISES

Before starting to do any serious stretching, it is important to do some warm-up exercises. They will ensure that your muscles are warmed and loosened and will help to prevent any strain. These gentle exercises can also be carried out on their own at any time if you are feeling stiff.

SHRUGGING SHOULDERS

1

2

ARM CIRCLING

1

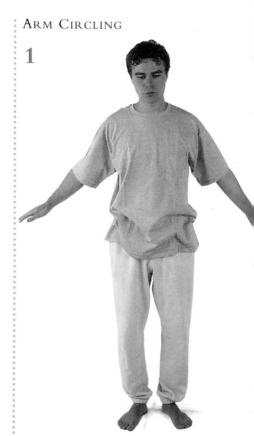

▲ Stand upright with your feet slightly apart and your shoulders relaxed.

▲ Lift your shoulders up as high as they will go, then let them fall down again. Repeat a few times.

▲ Wheel your arms around from the shoulders in slow, large circles.

Squats

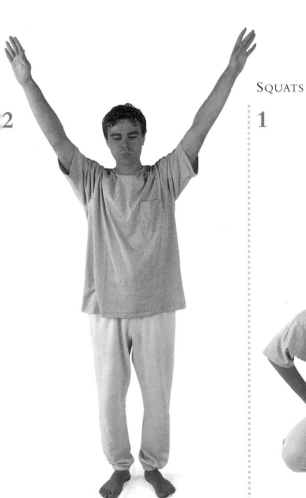

2

▲ Do this a few times going backwards, then repeat circling your arms forwards.

1

▲ Stand with your feet slightly apart, hands on hips. Go slowly down into a squatting position.

2

▲ Slowly return to a standing position, then repeat, always trying to keep your back upright.

LOOSE TWISTS

◀ In a standing position with feet comfortably apart and knees relaxed, swing your arms loosely backwards and forwards around your body.

▶ Keep your head and body facing forward all the time and keep your feet and pelvis still. Repeat a few times to loosen your arms and shoulders.

1

2

ARM-STRETCH BREATHING

1

2

▲ Stand with your arms straight out in front of you, at chest height. Take in a deep breath.

▲ As you inhale, move your arms out to the sides, keeping them raised. As you exhale, bring your arms back to the front. Repeat three or four times only.

CAT STRETCH

1

▲ Kneel on all fours, with your hands and knees shoulder-width apart. As you inhale, bring your head forward and slightly hollow the back.

2

▲ Now breathe out and, as you do so, arch the back upwards like a cat, allowing your head to drop down. Repeat a few times.

SIDEWAYS BEND

1

▲ Stand with your feet at least shoulder-width apart and your arms at your sides. Bend down to one side, trying not to twist.

2

▲ Slowly return to the upright and then bend to the other side. Straighten and repeat.

SHAKE

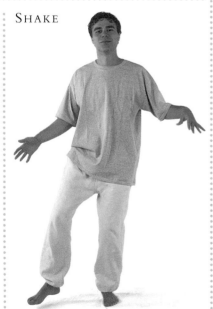

▲ Try to relax and let your whole body go completely floppy. Shake your limbs to release any tension.

FLEXIBILITY ENHANCERS

Stretching is not only important to encourage blood to flow back into tense, contracted muscles, but it also helps to increase suppleness and to relieve stress. When performing exercises to maintain flexible joints, you should aim to balance the movements: any forward bending of the spine, for instance, should be matched by following it with a backward bend movement.

FORWARD BEND

1

2

3

▲ Stand with your feet apart and knees slightly bent.

▲ Breathe in, lean forward and grasp your legs: try to hold your ankles if you can reach.

▲ Exhale, and as you do so straighten your legs; on breathing in let the knees flex again. Repeat.

THE BOW

1

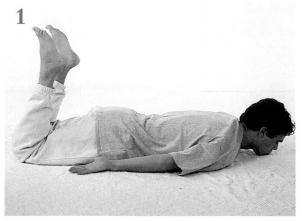

▲ Lie on your stomach, arms down by your sides and knees bent.

2

▲ Reaching behind you, try to grasp your feet with your hands.

3

▲ Lift your head and feet as far as is comfortable, and hold for a moment or two. Relax your body slowly to the floor and repeat twice.

CAUTION:

Some of the movements described are fairly challenging if you have not done any regular exercise for a while. You may find that to begin with you are not sufficiently flexible to achieve the final posture. Do not overdo or strain to do any of these movements; allow your body to lengthen and loosen gradually with regular practice.

THE PLOUGH

▲ Lie down on your back, with arms down by your sides and your hands flat on the floor for support. Raise your legs in the air.

CAUTION:
Like the Bow posture, this yoga position may be too difficult for some people, so do not strain too hard in trying to achieve the final position.

▲ Keep your legs going over your body towards your head as your bottom lifts off the floor.

▲ If possible, let your feet touch the floor behind your head.

▲ To return, flex your legs before letting your body come back over into the original position.

CHEST EXPANSION SEATED

This movement opens up the chest muscles and helps the flexibility of the spine.

1

2

▲ Sit in a cross-legged position, and clasp your hands together behind your back, raising your arms as far as is comfortable. To stretch the chest muscles further, breathe in as you raise your arms, then relax them slightly as you exhale.

▲ Inhale, then as you breathe out bend forward, your arms staying as high as possible to maintain the stretch. Uncurl your body slowly and return to the upright sitting position. With continued practice, you may be able to bring your arms into the vertical position. As with all stretches, never strain.

HEADACHE AND TENSION RELIEVERS

Many of us suffer from tension headaches and know that they begin with a feeling of pressure in the head or neck, or a taut sensation in the facial muscles. A few simple stretches can help to relieve this muscular tension and prevent it leading on to a severe headache. They can be done almost anywhere.

SIDEWAYS NECK STRETCH

1

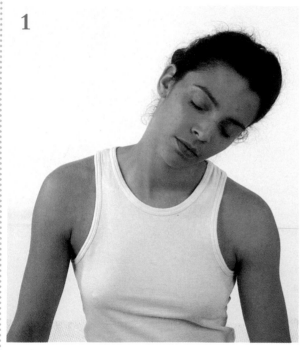

2

▲ Slowly stretch your head down to one side, feeling the pull in the neck muscles. Return the head to the upright position and repeat on the other side.

▲ To make this stretch of the neck muscles more effective, use your hands to give extra leverage. Place one hand under your chin and the other on top of your head; as you stretch sideways exert a steady pressure with both hands to add to the movement. Change hands and repeat on the other side.

HEAD TO CHEST

▲ Lower your head towards your chest, feeling the pull on the back of the neck. Hold at your furthest stretch before slowly raising the head again. Repeat two or three times.

LION POSTURE

▲ To stretch the facial muscles and release tension, open your mouth as wide as possible and push out your tongue. At the same time, open your eyes into as wide a stare as you can manage. Hold for a moment or two, then relax. Repeat a couple of times.

SEMICIRCLE ROTATION

1

▲ Turn the head to one side, then steadily rotate it in a semicircular movement, letting the chin drop down across the chest.

2

▲ Dropping the head backwards compresses the neck, so it is best not to make this a full circle rotation. Repeat, going back in the opposite direction.

21

SHOULDER TENSION

1

2

▲ In a kneeling position, interlink your fingers and raise your arms above your head.

▲ Stretch up as far as is comfortable and hold for a moment. Repeat three times.

POSTURE ENHANCERS

One of the benefits of an exercise system such as yoga is the increase in grace and poise that comes from improving your posture. Holding yourself properly can help you to look and feel younger, and reduce muscle strain. Try these stretches to help you regain your natural postural integrity.

STANDING TWIST

1

2

▲ Stand with feet slightly apart and arms raised straight out in front of you. Slowly twist your body to one side, keeping your feet firmly steady on the floor.

▲ Return to the centre and repeat on the other side. You can gain added benefit by keeping your feet together and rising up on to tip-toe before twisting.

RISHI'S POSTURE

1

2

3

▲ Stand with your feet shoulder-width apart, and hold your arms out in front of you.

▲ Bend over, sliding one hand down the inside of the same leg, while the other arm points up.

▲ Reach as far as is comfortable, then slowly return to the upright and repeat on the other side.

TREE

ARM AND LEG

1

▲ Stand on one leg and bend the other knee, raising the foot so that it rests on the inner thigh of the supporting leg. Raise the arms and hold the stretch, then repeat with the other leg.

2

▲ You can either place your palms together above your head, or raise the hands aloft.

▲ Stand on one leg and bend the other leg up behind you. Grasp the foot with the same hand and raise the other arm to point to the sky. Pull up on the foot and stretch up with the raised arm. Hold the stretch, then repeat with the other leg and arm.

TENSION AND BACKACHE RELIEVERS

The most common cause of lost time at work is backache. In the great majority of cases, back trouble is the result of chronic tensions, which build up in the back region. Tired, tight muscles are also much more prone to strain or injury. The stretches that we show here are intended to aid flexibility of the spine, but if you already suffer from back pain or an injury, seek professional advice.

COBRA

▲ Lie on your front, with your arms bent so that your hands are under your shoulders, palms facing down.

▲ Slowly lift your head and push down on your arms to help raise your trunk. Exhale as you raise your body.

▲ If you can, tilt your head backwards and stretch up and back as far as possible. Hold briefly, then relax and lower your body back down. Repeat.

BOTTOM RAISE

CAUTION:
Some of these stretches are quite difficult yoga postures: never force any movements or try to stretch too far.

▲ Lie on your back with your knees bent and feet flat on the floor, arms down by your sides.

▲ Push up with your bottom, lifting it and holding at the furthest limit. Lower, relax and repeat.

SIMPLE TWIST

1

▲ Sit on the floor with your legs straight out in front of you.

2

▲ Bend one leg and place the foot on the floor across the other knee.

3

▲ With your opposite arm, reach around the bent leg to catch hold of the straight leg, then twist your body. Relax and repeat on the other side.

FULL TWIST

1

▲ If you find the previous movement fairly easy, try to get a little more leverage on your lower spine by bending one leg so that the foot is resting on the inner thigh of the other leg.

2

▲ Bring this leg over the first one, then grasp your foot with the other arm.

3

▲ Twist as far around as you find comfortable, hold, then relax. Swop over your legs and repeat twisting to the other side.

BENDING TWIST

▶ Stand with your feet shoulder-width apart and your arms straight out to the sides.

▶ Bending forward, try to touch your foot, or the floor in front of it if you can, with your opposite hand. Slowly uncurl and return to the starting position. Repeat on the other side.

1

2

TRIANGLE

1

2

3

▲ Stand with your feet shoulder-width apart and your arms stretched out to the sides.

▲ Bend down to one side without twisting your body, letting the opposite arm rise in the air.

▲ Stretch the raised arm, look up and hold. Slowly straighten and repeat on the other side.

SLOUCH STRETCH

1

▲ Sit on a tall stool so that your feet are off the floor. Hands behind your back, slouch so that your back is rounded, with your head lowered towards your chest.

2

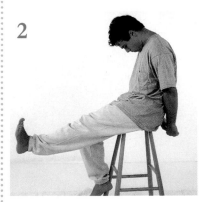

▲ Flex one foot, and lift the leg to straighten it if possible. Release the leg, relax, then repeat a few times. Repeat with the other leg.

LOCUST

1

▲ Lie on your stomach, with your arms down by your sides and your feet together.

2

▲ Keeping your upper body on the floor, try to raise both legs off the floor together, keeping them as straight as is comfortable. Lower the legs, relax for a moment and repeat. Do not strain too hard to have perfectly straight legs; as you become more supple this will be easier to achieve.

CHEST HUG

1

▲ To complete this sequence of exercises, relieve any strain in the back by lying on your back with legs bent up and hands clasped around the knees.

2

▲ Lift your head and hug your legs into your chest, hold, then relax. Take care not to strain your neck when lifting your head.

BREATHING AND BLOOD FLOW ENHANCERS

Chronic tensions and anxiety can often make us feel very tight across the chest, so that it becomes difficult to breathe deeply. To improve breathing and blood flow to the chest muscles and lungs, use these stretching exercises on a regular basis. Expanding the chest enables the lungs to fill with more oxygen, which will, in turn, nourish all the cells in the body, including the respiratory organs themselves.

COMPLETE BREATH

1

▲ Stand with feet together, arms by your sides.

2

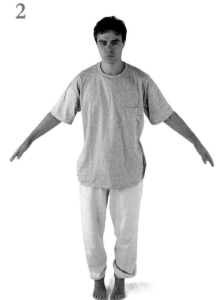

▲ Slowly take a deep breath, and as you do so raise your arms out to the side.

3

▲ Raise your arms until they meet over your head, and at the same time rise up on to your toes. As you exhale, slowly return to the original position. Repeat this exercise two or three times only.

BACKWARDS BEND, KNEELING

1

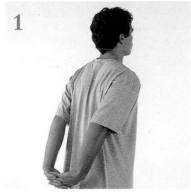

▲ Kneel on the floor, sitting on your heels. Place your hands on the floor just behind you.

2

▲ Raise your trunk to arch up and back as you inhale. Hold for a moment, then sink back into the kneeling position as you exhale.

BACKWARDS BEND, STANDING

▲ Stand with hands on hips. Breathe in, then exhale as you bend backwards from the waist. Avoid if you have back problems.

CHEST EXPANSION

1

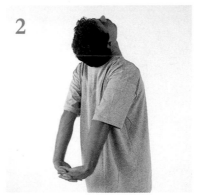

▲ Stand with feet together and clasp your hands together behind your back.

2

▲ Try to raise your arms a little, leaning back slightly. Then lean forwards as far as possible.

3

▲ Keep your arms lifted as high as is comfortable. Slowly straighten up, relax and repeat.

31

TIRED AND ACHING LEG REVIVERS

Standing or sitting, most of us spend too long each day with our legs stuck in fixed positions. Stiffness of the lower limbs from inactivity or tension can make us feel generally tired. Legs benefit greatly from being stretched, keeping them toned and supple. These exercises will prevent the legs, thighs and lower back from getting too tense, and help you to move freely.

ALTERNATE LEG PULLS

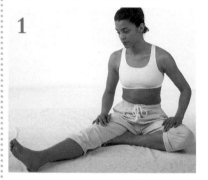

1

◀ Sit on the floor, with one leg out straight and the other bent so that the foot rests on the inner thigh of the extended leg.

▶ Lean forward and clasp the straight leg as far down as is comfortable; pull your chest down a little further and hold for a moment. Change legs and repeat.

2

FULL LEG PULLS

1

2

▲ The previous stretch can be extended by starting with both legs straight out in front of you.

▲ Lean forward and hold the legs with both hands; pull yourself down a little further and hold for a moment. If this is difficult, bend the legs slightly.

SIDE LEG RAISE

1

2

◀ Lie on your side with your legs and body in a straight line. Support your head with one hand and place your free hand on the floor in front of you for balance.

◀ Without twisting your hips, steadily raise the upper leg as far as is comfortable. Hold, then lower slowly. Repeat with the other leg.

CAT STRETCH

1

2

▲ Kneel on all fours with your hands and knees shoulder-width apart. Raise your head and look straight ahead.

▲ Breathe in, and as you exhale lift and arch your back. Hold for a moment before relaxing back into the original position. Inhale, then repeat.

KNEE AND THIGH STRETCH

▲ Sit on the floor and bend your legs so that the soles of your feet are together. Hold the feet with your hands and try to pull the feet a little closer to your body. Let the knees drop down towards the floor, hold the stretch, then bring up your knees to relax. Repeat.

LEG OVER

▲ Lie on your back, with legs out straight. Raise one leg as close to the vertical as is comfortable, then move it across the body, keeping your hips on the floor.

▲ Allow the leg to go as far over as possible, then slowly return to the original position. Repeat with the other leg.

▼ CAUTION: Do not strain yourself with this movement – it works on lots of muscles at the same time.

BACK PUSH-UP

▲ Lie on your back with your knees bent and your feet on the floor, hip-width apart. Place your hands on the floor by your shoulders.

▲ Push up with your hands and feet, arching your back at the same time. Hold for a moment, then lower your body back to the floor.

SIT UP/LIE DOWN

1

▲ Sit on the floor with both legs straight out in front of you.

2

▲ Slowly lower your back to the floor, then start to bend the legs and raise them off the floor.

3

▲ As you raise the legs, straighten them until they are as close to the vertical as possible.

4

▲ Keeping the legs straight, slowly lower them to the floor.

5

▲ Continue the movement by sitting up and clasping your legs with your hands to bend forwards. Slowly return to the original sitting position.

TENSION AND POOR CIRCULATION

When our legs and arms become very tired, either through general tension or muscle fatigue, the contraction of the muscles can lead to poor circulation to the extremities. This can become a vicious cycle, as the restricted blood flow fails to nourish the muscles adequately, leading them to stay in a more contracted state. One or two simple stretches can help to restore blood supply to the area as well as relieving tight, cramped muscles.

CALF STRETCH

HAMSTRING STRETCH

▲ Sit on the floor with one leg out in front of you; if possible, lean forward and grasp the foot with your hand. Pull the foot gently towards you, feeling the tightness in the calf. If you are unable to hold the foot in this position, try doing this stretch with the leg slightly bent. Repeat with the other leg.

▶ Stand upright and lift one leg off the floor. Clasp your hands behind the knee to pull the leg towards your chest. Relax, then repeat with the other leg.

CALF AND FOOT EXERCISE

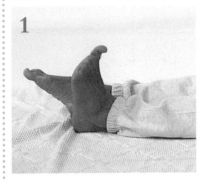

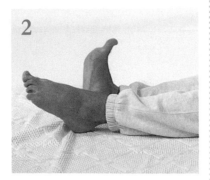

▲ Sit on the floor with both legs straight out in front of you, then alternately flex and extend each foot.

▲ You should have one foot flexed while the other is extended, and vice versa.

FINGER PULLS

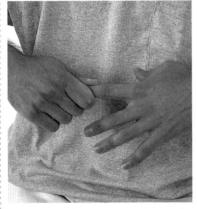

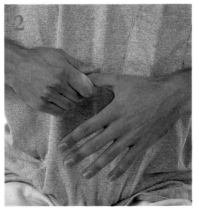

▲ Hands often store tension and feel tight: to help ease out tension, take one finger of one hand and grasp it firmly with the other hand. Give it a steady pull.

▲ Repeat for each finger in turn. Then swap hands and repeat.

THIGH STRETCH

▲ The muscles in the front of the thighs, the quadriceps, can be stretched by standing on one leg and bending the other leg up behind you. Clasp the foot with your hand and pull it further up towards the back. Hold, then relax. Repeat with the other leg.

REVITALIZING PASSIVE STRETCHES

One of the nicest and most effective ways to ease out really tired, tense muscles after a stressful day at work is by means of passive stretching. In these exercises, someone else helps your body to extend and stretch that little bit further. Assisting with these revitalizing stretches can be a very positive way to help your partner unwind and release any stored tension. They can do it for you next time you are tired and tense.

HEAD TO CHEST

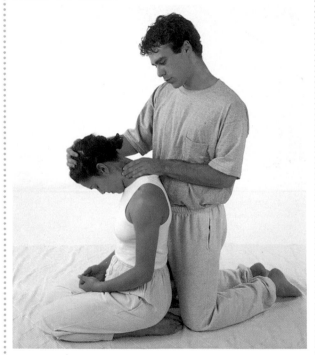

▲ With your partner kneeling up, place one hand on the back of the neck. As your partner lowers his/her head towards the chest, use your other hand to give added resistance by pulling down on the neck muscles.

NECK TRACTION

▲ Ask your partner to lie down, and sit or kneel at his/her head. Cradle the head in your hands and gently pull towards you to stretch the neck.

CAUTION:
Do not over-stretch the neck, and avoid this exercise if your partner has any injury or discomfort in the neck joints (for which they should seek professional advice).

ARM PULLS

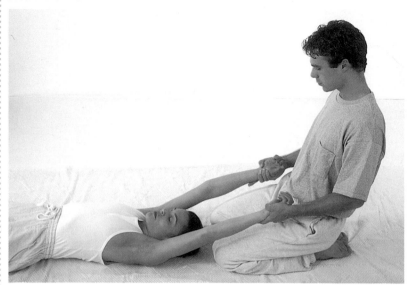

◀ With your partner lying down, take both wrists in your hands and bring the arms over the head. Steadily pull towards you, but do not cause discomfort or pain in the shoulder joint. Hold briefly and repeat.

LEG PULLS

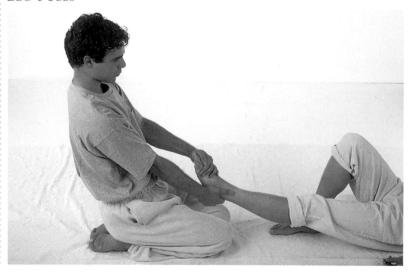

◀ Finally, with your partner lying down take one ankle in your hands and give a steady pull with the leg slightly raised off the floor. Hold and repeat, then do the same to the other leg.

INSTANT FATIGUE REVITALIZERS

Chronic stress and tension can easily lead to fatigue and exhaustion. If you find that your memory and concentration seem to be worse than usual and that stress leads to constant tiredness, then you may find these exercises, which aim to improve circulation to the brain, helpful.

SHOULDER STAND

1

▲ Lie on your back, with your legs straight and your arms by your sides. Raise your legs until they are vertical. Continue to lift your legs over your head while raising your bottom off the floor.

2

▲ Support your lower back with your hands and slowly try to bring your back and legs to the vertical position: do not strain.

3

▲ Hold for a few moments, then return in the same way to the original position.

CAUTION:
Do not do any exercises which involve an inverted posture if you have high blood pressure or an over-active thyroid gland, without first seeking medical advice.

FISH POSTURE

CAUTION: Avoid strain on your neck: do not do this if you have neck problems.

◄ Lie flat on your back.

◄ Arch your back until the top of your head is resting on the floor. Hold, then relax.

LEG CLASP

▲ Stand upright with your feet together. Bending forward, clasp your hands behind your legs, as far down as is comfortable.

▲ Steadily pull your head towards your legs. Go only as far as you can without strain. Hold for a few moments. Then slowly uncurl and return to the upright.

BACKWARDS BEND, STANDING

▲ Stand with your hands on your hips, feet slightly apart. Breathe in, then exhale as you bend backwards from the waist. Do not go further than is comfortable, and avoid this stretch if you suffer from back problems.

41

RISHI'S POSTURE

▲ Stand with your feet shoulder-width apart, and your arms raised in front of you.

▲ Twist your body and bend over so that one hand slides down the inside of the same leg, while the other arm points up to the sky.

▲ Look up at the raised arm. Reach as far down the leg as is comfortable, then slowly return to an upright position and repeat, bending the other way.

SIMPLE STRETCH

◀ Place several cushions or a low stool on the floor and lie on your back so that the cushions support you in the lumbar area, with your head lower than your pelvis. Relax in this position. Using a stool will raise your bottom higher, and even more blood will flow back to the brain. Make sure that there is no strain on your back.

DOG POSE

1

▲ Stand with your feet slightly apart, then place your hands on the floor, as far in front of you as you can manage comfortably.

2

▲ Try to straighten your legs. As you do so, arch your back, stretching up into an inverted V-shape; hold for a while, relax and repeat.

CHILD'S POSE

◄ Finally, rest and relax your body by kneeling on the floor and bending forward to place your head on the floor, with your arms down by your side. This position can be relaxing after any back bends.

CAUTION:
If you have suffered a back injury, seek medical advice before doing these stretches. Always stop any exercise immediately if you feel acute discomfort.

ANXIETY AND TENSION RELIEVERS

Anxiety and worry are feelings that we all experience at times; problems arise when these inner tensions become an overriding factor in our lives. Throughout this book, you will find stretching and yoga postures that help to ease muscular tension – this in turn has a calming effect on our minds, and regular practice of stretches can help in reducing the impact of stress. Yoga itself is much more than just physical exercises, however. It is a whole philosophy of life, and an important part of yoga practice is meditation. There are many different approaches to meditation, from using visualization techniques to repeating mantras. Whichever method of calming the mind you adopt, here are a few simple exercises to help the process.

LOTUS
The lotus position is a relaxed, stable posture for meditation. The simpler version is the half-lotus.

1

2

▲ Sit with one leg bent so that the foot rests on the inner thigh of the other leg. Bend the second leg and place the foot on top of the opposite thigh. Keep the spine upright so that you are not straining the body.

▲ For the full lotus, the first leg should be bent with the foot on top of the other thigh, and the second leg bent so that the foot goes over the other leg on to the opposite thigh. Hold for as long as is comfortable.

ALTERNATE NOSTRIL BREATHING

Meditation and calming of the mind are made easier by using regular, quiet, breathing exercises.

1

▲ Place your hand on your fore-head, with thumb and third finger reaching down to close off each nostril.

2

▲ Relax your thumb, and breathe in through that nostril; pinch it closed again, then release the finger to allow the exhalation through the other nostril.

3

▲ Breathe in through this nostril, close and then relax the thumb again to exhale that side. Continue to use alternate nostrils, breathing calmly and slowly.

DIRECTING ENERGY

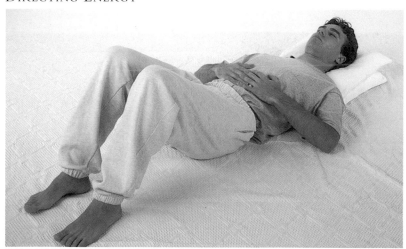

◀ Greater relaxation can take place by focusing the mind. Lie on your back and become aware of any area of tension. Place your hands on this area, and imagine feeling a sense of relaxation flow through your hands into this part of your body. Repeat for any other tense spots.

ABDOMINAL TENSION RELIEVERS

We tend to hold much of our tension in our abdomen, especially if we bottle up feelings. Even simple muscular tension can leave us less flexible around the waist; exercises to reduce stiffness and increase flexibility in the abdominal region are useful in many situations.

SIDEWAYS BENDS

1

▲ Stand with feet apart and hands on hips. Bend down to one side, trying not to twist at the same time.

2

▲ Slowly return to the upright position and then bend to the other side. Repeat a few times.

ROLL TWIST

▲ Stand with feet apart and hands on hips. Keeping the legs and hips still, roll your upper body around in a clockwise circle.

▲ Move slowly and bend only as far as is comfortable.

▲ Repeat the roll in the opposite direction.

ABDOMINAL MOVEMENTS

◀ Either sit cross-legged or kneel, and place your hands on your waist or thighs. Breathe out completely.

▶ Without inhaling, pull in your abdomen as far as you can, then "snap" it in and out up to five times before taking a breath. Relax for a few moments, breathing freely, before repeating.

LEG OVER

1

◀ Lie on your back, with legs out straight. Raise one leg as close to the vertical as is comfortable, then move it across the body, keeping your hips on the floor.

▶ Push the leg as far over as possible, then slowly return to the original position. Repeat with the other leg.

2

LYING TWISTS

▲ Lie on your back with your hands behind your head and legs together, knees slightly bent.

▲ Twist the legs from one side to the other, keeping as much of the back and hips on the floor as possible.

SIT UP/LIE DOWN

1

▲ Sit on the floor with both legs straight out in front of you.

2

▲ Slowly lie back down, then start to bend the legs and raise them off the floor.

3

▲ As you raise the legs, straighten them until they are as close to the vertical as possible. Hold, then, keeping the legs straight, slowly lower them to the floor.

4

▲ To finish the sequence, sit up, and then bend forwards, clasping your legs with your hands. Slowly return to the original sitting position.

OFFICE TENSIONS AND STIFF MUSCLES

For people who spend their working day sitting at a desk, whether at home or in an office, it is very easy to get stiff and aching muscles. As we get tired, our posture suffers and we can find ourselves becoming round-shouldered. Many office chairs are not good for the posture, and long hours spent staring at a computer screen can give our neck, upper and lumbar back muscles a very hard time. Regular breaks help: get up and walk around every now and then, and also try to loosen your body using some of these simple stretches while sitting at your desk.

ARM AND BACK STRETCH

▲ Link your hands together, palms away from your body, and push your arms straight out in front of you. Hold for a couple of moments, relax and repeat.

ARM AND CHEST STRETCH

▲ Link your hands together behind your back, over the top of the chair, and lift your arms slightly. Push away from your body, hold, then repeat.

FOREARM STRETCH

▲ Lift your arms straight out to the sides and stretch them out.

▲ Alternately flex and extend your hands. Feel the pull on the upper and lower sides of your forearms as you do so.

BACK AND SHOULDER STRETCH

▲ Stretch your arms up in the air over your head. As you take a breath, arch your back slightly. Relax with the exhalation and repeat a couple of times.

POSTURE CLASP

▲ Take one arm behind your back and bend it upwards, with the hand reaching towards the opposite shoulder. With your other arm raised and bent downwards over your shoulder, try to clasp your fingers, or even your hands, together. Hold for a short time, then repeat with your hands in the opposite positions.

SEATED CAT STRETCH

1

▲ Pull the chair back from the desk slightly to give yourself more room, then bend forward and clasp your ankles.

2

▲ Arch your back to stretch, relax and repeat.

CALF STRETCH

▲ Sit fairly upright, then lift and straighten each leg alternately.

▲ Flex the foot to stretch the calf muscle. Repeat a few times.

NECK TWISTS

▲ Slowly turn your head to one side, feeling the extension in the neck muscles.

▲ Repeat, turning the head from side to side.

SHOULDER RELEASE

▲ Finally, link your fingers together and stretch your arms high above your head.

WAKING-UP STRETCHES

Do you wake up feeling stiff and tired, maybe even still a little tense from the stresses of yesterday? A few simple stretches can make you feel more refreshed and better able to face a new morning. Stretching gets the blood flowing, bringing oxygen to your body's cells, and helps you to wake up.

COMPLETE BREATH

1

▲ Stand with feet together, arms down and head bowed.

2

▲ Slowly take a deep breath, and as you do so lift your arms out to the side and raise your head.

3

▲ Keep raising your arms until they meet over your head, and at the same time rise up onto your toes. As you exhale, slowly return to your original position. Repeat two or three times only.

FORWARD–BACKWARD BEND

1

2

▲ Stand with your feet slightly apart and your hands on your hips. As you inhale, bend back from the waist.

▲ Now exhale, bending forward as you do so. Slowly return to your upright position, relax and repeat, holding each stretch.

STANDING TWIST

1

▲ Stand with your feet shoulder-width apart and arms straight out to the sides.

2

▲ Twist from the waist to one side, then twist around to the other side. Make the movements slowly and freely.

CAT STRETCH

1

▲ Kneel on the floor and curl up into a ball.

2

▲ Now move out onto all fours, hollowing your back slightly as you inhale.

3

▲ As you exhale, arch your back, hold and relax. Return to your original position and repeat.

TRAVELLERS' STRETCHES

If your work involves a lot of travel, whether by car, train or plane, you will be uncomfortably aware of how stiff you can feel at the end of the day. Long journeys place quite a strain on our bodies, and we can arrive tired, tense and fatigued even aside from any mental strain which may accompany the trip. If the journey is going to take several hours, try to take frequent short breaks. Doing some simple stretching exercises during or shortly after a journey can relieve tensions and refresh both body and mind.

SIDEWAYS BENDS

HAMSTRING STRETCH

▲ Stand with feet shoulder-width apart, arms outstretched. Bend down to one side, trying not to twist the body.

▲ Slowly return to the upright position and then bend to the other side. Straighten and repeat.

▲ Stand upright and lift one leg. Clasp your knee, then pull the leg up towards your chest. Relax, then repeat with the other leg.

THIGH STRETCH

▲ Bend one leg up behind you. Clasp the foot and pull it further up towards the lower back. Feel the stretch on the thigh. Relax and repeat with the other leg.

FORWARD–BACKWARD BEND

1

▲ Stand with your feet slightly apart, hands on your hips. As you inhale, bend back from the waist.

2

▲ Bend forward as you exhale. Slowly return to the upright, relax and repeat, holding each stretch.

BACKWARDS BEND

▶ Stand with your hands on your hips, feet slightly apart. Breathe in, then exhale as you bend backwards from the waist. Return to the upright as you breathe in.

CAUTION:
Do not go further than is comfortable, and avoid this stretch if you have back problems. After a journey, you can be quite stiff and it may be beneficial to shake your whole body before starting.

HIP AND PELVIC TENSION

The pelvic basin is an important area in the body, containing the reproductive organs as well as the bladder and the lower part of the bowel. Stretching exercises can benefit this region; they help to improve blood flow to and from the area and tone all these organs. The shape of the pelvic structure means that blood can pool in this area, and the stretches suggested here can relieve congestion, among other things helping to ease period pains or aiding better prostate function.

SIT-UPS

1

▲ Lie on your back with your legs bent, feet apart, and your hands behind your head. Breathe in.

2

▲ As you exhale, lift your head off the floor as far as is comfortable; hold for a moment, then relax. Repeat.

TWISTING SIT-UPS

1

▲ Lie on your back as before. Inhale, then as you breathe out raise your head and twist, at the same time raising your leg so that opposite elbow and knee move towards each other.

2

▲ Relax, then repeat, twisting the other way.

PARTIAL TWIST

1

▲ Sit on the floor with your legs straight out in front of you.

2

▲ Bend one leg, and place the foot across the other leg.

3

▲ With your other arm reach around the bent leg to catch hold of the straight leg, then twist your body as illustrated. Relax and repeat on the other side.

KNEE AND THIGH STRETCH

▲ Sitting on the floor, bend the legs so that the soles of the feet are together. Hold the feet with your hands, and try to pull them a little closer to your body. Let the knees drop down towards the floor, hold the stretch, relax and repeat.

BUTTERFLY POSTURE

▲ The knee and thigh stretch can also be done while lying down. Lie on your back and bend your legs so that the soles of the feet are together. Allow the knees to sink towards the floor and hold for several moments. This can be useful during pregnancy, and by stimulating blood flow it can also help men with prostate problems.

BOTTOM RAISE

◀ Lie on your back with your knees bent and feet flat on the floor. Put your arms down by your sides for support.

▶ Push up with your bottom, lifting it off the floor and holding at the furthest limit. Lower, relax and repeat.

SHOULDER STAND

CHEST HUG

▲ Lie on your back, with your legs straight. Raise your legs until they are vertical, then continue to lift them towards your head while raising your bottom off the floor. Support your lower back with your hands.

▲ Try to bring your back and legs to the vertical position, but do not strain. Hold for a few moments, then return in the same way to the original position.

▲ At the end of these exercises, relieve any strain in the lumbar area by lying on your back with legs bent up, hands clasped around the knees. Lift your head and hug your knees into your chest, hold and relax.

WINDING-DOWN STRETCHES

At the end of a long day it can be easy to fall into bed with many muscles still being held tight and contracted and the mental stresses of the day's work weighing on your mind; this can lead to disturbed sleep, or worse still you may not even be able to get to sleep. To help your mind and body release the day's tensions and prepare for a sound night's sleep, spend a few quiet minutes doing these winding-down stretching exercises.

NECK STRETCH

▲ Slowly stretch your head down to one side, feeling the pull in the neck muscles. Return the head to the upright position and repeat on the other side. Move slowly and hold each stretch for a moment.

LION POSTURE

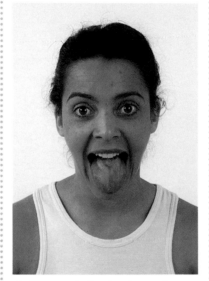

▲ To stretch the facial muscles and release tension, open your mouth as wide as possible and push out your tongue. At the same time, open your eyes into as wide a stare as you can manage. Hold for a moment or two, then relax. Repeat a couple of times.

FORWARD BEND

▲ Stand with feet apart and knees slightly bent. Lean forward and let your arms hang freely. Then grasp your legs: try to hold your ankles if you can reach. Exhale, and as you do so straighten your legs; on breathing in let the knees flex again. Repeat.

SQUATS

1   **2**   **3**

▲ Stand with your feet slightly apart and raise your arms.

▲ Lift your hands above your head, palms touching, and at the same time, rise up onto your toes.

▲ Slowly lower yourself into the squatting position, trying to keep your back straight. Slowly return to standing, then repeat.

STANDING TWIST

1

2

◀ Stand with your feet shoulder-width apart and arms raised straight out in front of you. Slowly twist your body to one side.

▶ Return to the centre, then twist from the waist to the other side. Make the movements slowly and freely.

BACKWARDS BEND, KNEELING

▶ Kneel on the floor, sitting on your heels. Place your hands on the floor just behind you, and raise your trunk to arch up and back as you inhale. Hold for a moment and then sink back into the kneeling position as you exhale.

INDEX

Picture Credits
Sue Atkinson (direction Mira
Mehta) p. 6 and p. 8.